Copyright © 2016 by Anu Taranath. All rights reserved. No part of this book may be transmitted or reproduced in any form by any means without permission in writing.

ISBN-13: 978-0692792070
ISBN-10: 0692792074
First printing, November 2016

Let's WOW It Out:

simple drawings to explore big ideas

Anu Taranath & the WOWers

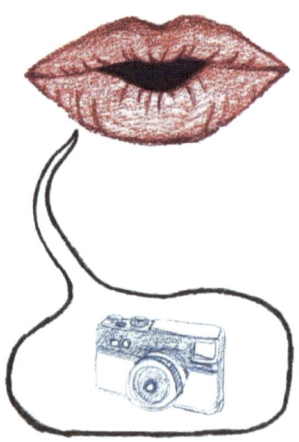

Dear Reader,

Are you looking for a simple way to approach complex ideas? A way to artistically engage with our world in an easy yet meaningful activity?

If you're a teacher, do you dream of new ways to encourage your students to express their ideas in an easily-accessible yet high-impact way?

And if you're a student, are you eager to try another learning approach that doesn't always revolve around words?

Welcome to *Let's WOW it Out: Simple Drawings to Explore Big Ideas*. We offer a fun and effective tool to better understand big ideas. Look inside to find rich examples of student artwork to inspire you!

Thank you for joining us!

Warmly,
The WOWers

Art is one of the best ways to get our hearts around the teachings that often get stuck in our heads. Creativity helps us move things from the "heady space" of knowing to "heart work" of practicing.

-Brené Brown

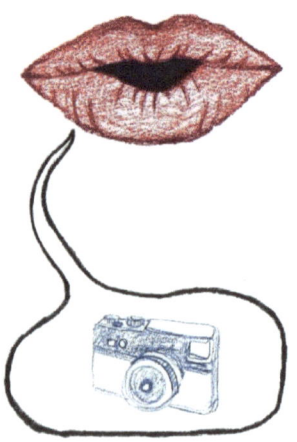

What's Inside

Introduction

Lenses: How We Understand

Journeys: How We Explore

Reflections: How We Unpack

What Else Can We WOW About?

Thank You

Meet the WOWers

Introduction

by Anu Taranath

Big Ideas Need New Assignments

As a university professor and study abroad program director, I teach about big global issues like power, privilege, identity, race, gender, sexuality, culture, colonialism, migration and world literature. While the big issues of our world are everywhere, I've found it's sometimes difficult to make them relevant to our smaller, more local lives. And so, I am always looking for new ways to engage my students in both the big and small ideas. Sometimes, stretching beyond what we know can be discomforting and can make us nervous. How do we best support students to stretch and learn while also keeping them grounded in creativity? This was the question I was asking myself when planning the latest iteration of the study abroad program I lead to India.

From Words to WOW

Like most teachers in the humanities, I am familiar with and rely on words as my main teaching and learning device. Most of my students— and indeed, most students across the US and broader world— are also familiar with and rely on words as they are asked to write the quintessential demonstration of their comprehension: the 5-page paper and essay. Words, of course, convey rich meaning. Words also demonstrate complex ideas in their most minute form. It's no wonder words reign supreme. I like the 5-page paper and essay as much as the next person. But words are sometimes too expected, and too, you know, wordy. What if words might not always be the best device to inspire creativity, new thoughts and daring connections? Might there be other ways to stretch our students' intellects?

Anyone can Art

My study abroad assistant Amy Hirayama and I wondered if there were less word-reliant ways to teach and learn about big ideas. Art, she said excitedly, and I panicked. Art? I squeaked. I knew nothing about art. How would I teach this kind of creativity to students if I, the teacher, understood so little of it?

Amy suggested I talk to a few others before letting my fears foreclose a good idea. I spoke with Otts Bolisay, a Seattle-based graphic artist, and he too assuaged my concerns. Amy and Otts helped me understand that just like we create new ideas by the process of writing, the artistic process of sketching and drawing can also open up new intellectual pathways and create novel connections. "You don't have to be an artist to use art," both friends said. "Just be open and see what happens."

Convinced and enthusiastic, Amy and I then brainstormed an assignment called "WOWs," acronym for "Word Of the Week," a way for my students to engage with our readings and discussion themes from a different, more artistic angle. Every week I would give them a new WOW prompt comprised of a word or phrase. Their task: to WOW the word or phrase into an image, drawing or sketch.

How we WOWed

What began as an unusual and tentative assignment quickly became the students' beloved friend, incorporated into the very ethos of our pre-departure class in Seattle and the study abroad program in India. WOWs grounded our conversations of big ideas into smaller chunks.

We WOWed big words like "colonialism" and "privilege," and phrases like "travel ethics" and "global feminism." I had students share their weekly WOWs with one another via a document camera, and submit to me a one-paragraph written explanation of their WOW to complement the image. WOWs reframed how we engaged with both the big and small ideas of our trip by giving us a new tool for engagement and expression. We WOWed often, and we learned an awful lot about the power of imagery and how we can say a lot without relying on words. And because we loved WOWs so much, we decided to create this book and share the WOW tool and our drawings with you.

Let's WOW it Out

This book presents a curated collection of artwork created by a group of U.S. undergraduate students before, during and after their journeys abroad. The students I led to India in 2015 were the first WOWers. Once we returned back to Seattle, we then opened our class to students who had studied abroad in and traveled through not only India but Nepal, Peru, Netherlands, Malaysia, Philippines, Tibet and Thailand. *Let's WOW It Out: Simple Drawings to Explore Big Ideas* presents a simple yet effective strategy to grapple with complex ideas. We invite you to put pen or pencil to paper and ask yourself: What will I WOW?

What Can a WOW Do?

Sort out
Clarify
Complicate
Process
Connect
Interpret
Navigate
Reflect
Express
Contextualize
Stretch
Bridge and
Illuminate ideas...

How are WOWs different than 5-page papers?

WOWs represent an innovative and different way of learning in schools and universities.

WOWs create quick visual impact and draw in audiences.

WOWs represent vulnerability since so much of the author/illustrator is splashed right there on the page.

WOWs allow you to show yourself in more holistic ways.

WOWs build on the research within ourselves by encouraging us to dig deep and find connections.

WOWs can be sparse or embellished depending on the artist's approach.

WOWs are meant to be shared.

WOWs start conversations.

WOWs are help create a horizontal camaraderie between people.

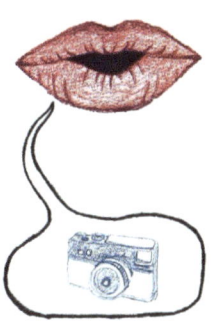

Lenses:
How We Understand

Art by Meili

Critical lenses guide the ways we engage, interpret, and analyze what we see, read, hear, feel and learn. Because so many of us are interested in issues of social justice, we wanted to approach our travels with a more informed lens. How has the world been divided and created by the histories of imperialism and colonialism? How do our different identities of race, gender and wealth, for example, shift our experiences of our communities both near and far? To better engage with these questions, we WOWed about feminism, colonialism and privilege. The critical awareness we developed helps us to see beyond the surface level to examine why things are the way they are, and to question how inequality and injustice persist. Perhaps through a process of introspection we can find points of connection with different people, different experiences, and different contexts around the world.

I wanted to portray colonialism as a form of gluttony: one nation consumes resources while exploiting others to the point of gross excess. -Maya

When we go abroad our conscious and unconscious cultural baggage travels with us, following us like an unshakeable shadow. Though we can't choose what privileges we arrive with, being aware of how our background informs and colors our experiences can help us make the most of our time overseas. -Ian

I first noticed my white privilege this summer while traveling internationally. While many airports gave South Asian families extra security screenings and pat-downs, officials always greeted me, a white male "tourist," with a smile, never questioning my intentions. These events inspired a WOW which explores different aspects of privilege. I highlighted privilege as an unearned tool with exclusive access, an advantage that directly relates to someone else's disadvantage or oppression, and as a possession that can go completely unnoticed by the owner. -Trent

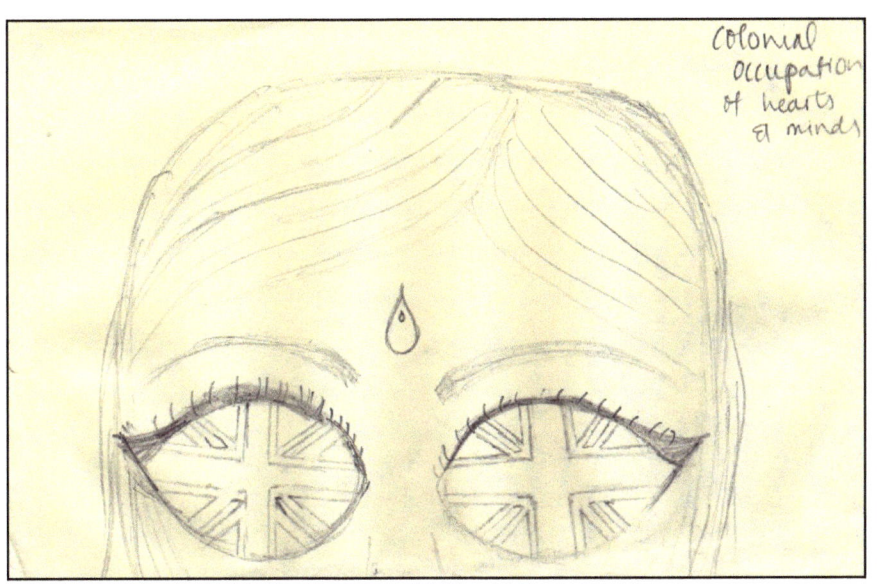

While some colonized peoples are legally liberated, many still endure colonial occupation of the heart and mind. A history of colonial "us vs. them" ideology alienates the "them," deeming them disposable, invalid, and irrelevant. This image depicts the heartbreaking effects of an internalized notion of inferiority that continually haunts communities of colonized peoples. -Ruby

Among a sea of brunettes, each strand of my blonde hair acted as a constant reminder of my privilege within Lima. Brushing through these tangled strands, I realized how I was granted more respect, access, and admiration through the language that greeted me. -Haley

Feminism is about equality, yet those who tend to the trees of patriarchy find their power in phrases like, "No respectable woman is out after 8."
These trees don't grow to protect. They hide and trap women in their branches and roots. -Karan

The crow is made up of
fingerprints representing a
strong personal identity that
remains after oppression and
colonialism. The bird itself is
traditionally a symbol of "power
for deep inner transformation."
-Stefanie

While women share the common characteristic of being female, this commonality gets disregarded when women get categorized based on societal power hierarchies that cause certain groups of women to be viewed as "other". It is critical for women to focus on viewing all women from all cultural identities based on similarities rather than differences (as if they were looking through a mirror), and join forces against patriarchy and other shared systematic injustices.   -Meili

I read a short story in which the heroine braided a razor blade into her hair so that when her attacker grabbed it, she would not be defenseless. Sometimes, empowerment is as passive and as potent as a razor blade hidden in a braid. Beginning to fight, no matter how small the resistance, can be the beginning of something greater. -Anna

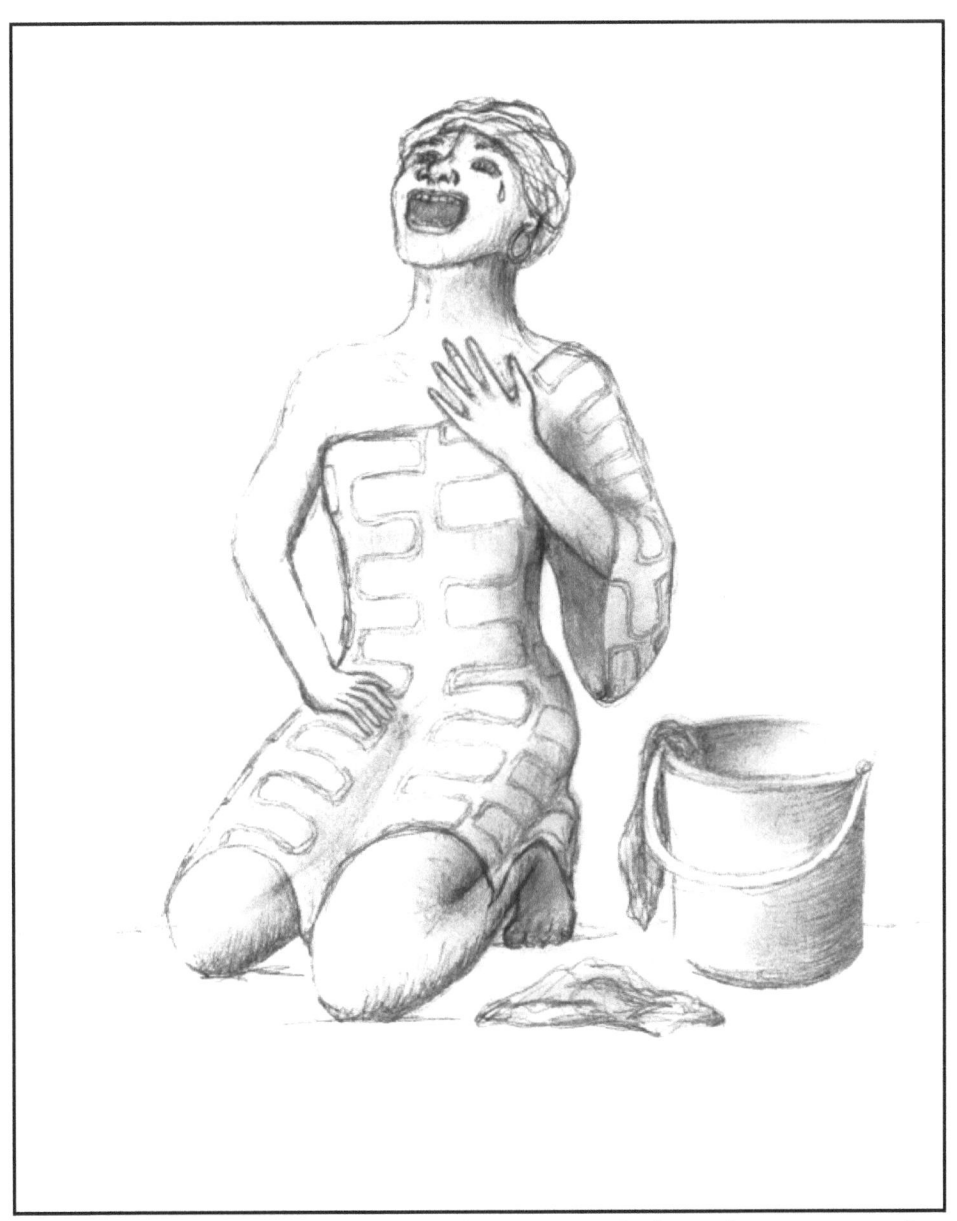

"Sisterarchy": global sisterhood in the eyes of Western feminists. The term is sisterarchy, and not sisterhood due to a hierarchy in the group where Western women are at the top. The woman in this picture is laughing and crying at the irony of the white woman telling her they are equal in their fight against patriarchy - that they are in the same sisterhood. -Chloe

TIPS (Things, Ideas, People and Self) is not just a way to look at the world, it's a way to live your life. Things are here to distract us, but ideas will set you free. There's all types of people out there, so be the change you want to see. -Spencer

Journeys: How We Explore

Art by Maya

As we move through the world, our own lives touch the lives of those we meet. We exchange stories, a few laughs, and sometimes, even tears. As we travel to see and hear more beyond our own familiar experiences, we bear witness to new sights, sounds and smells. We know that travel expands us in innumerable ways, but sometimes, we too must ask ourselves: just because we can go somewhere else, should we? The questions we ask encourage us to dig deeper, not only about the ethics of our journey, but ourselves as well. Who are we, we might ask? What are the things, ideas and people who have helped shape us? Journeys stretch us, and through this process, we find and make joy.

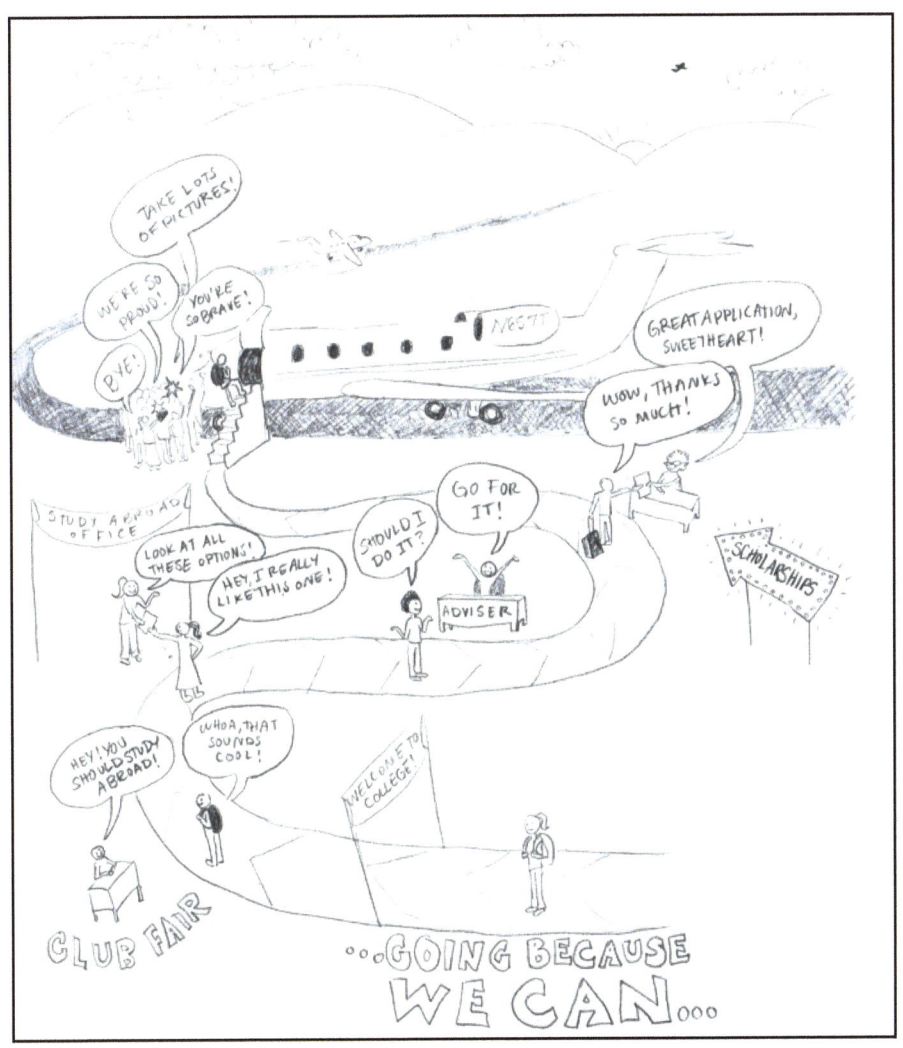

On my journey through the University, I have been constantly bombarded with encouragement to study abroad from many different sources. Studying abroad can be a transformative and amazing experience, but should the resounding "GO" that echoes throughout the University be balanced out by questioning the act of going? -Maya

While abroad I wanted to immerse myself in a new culture while also holding onto my roots. I viewed Amsterdam through the lens of Seattle, therefore not forgetting my old self in the process of exploring my new self in a different setting. -Elysse

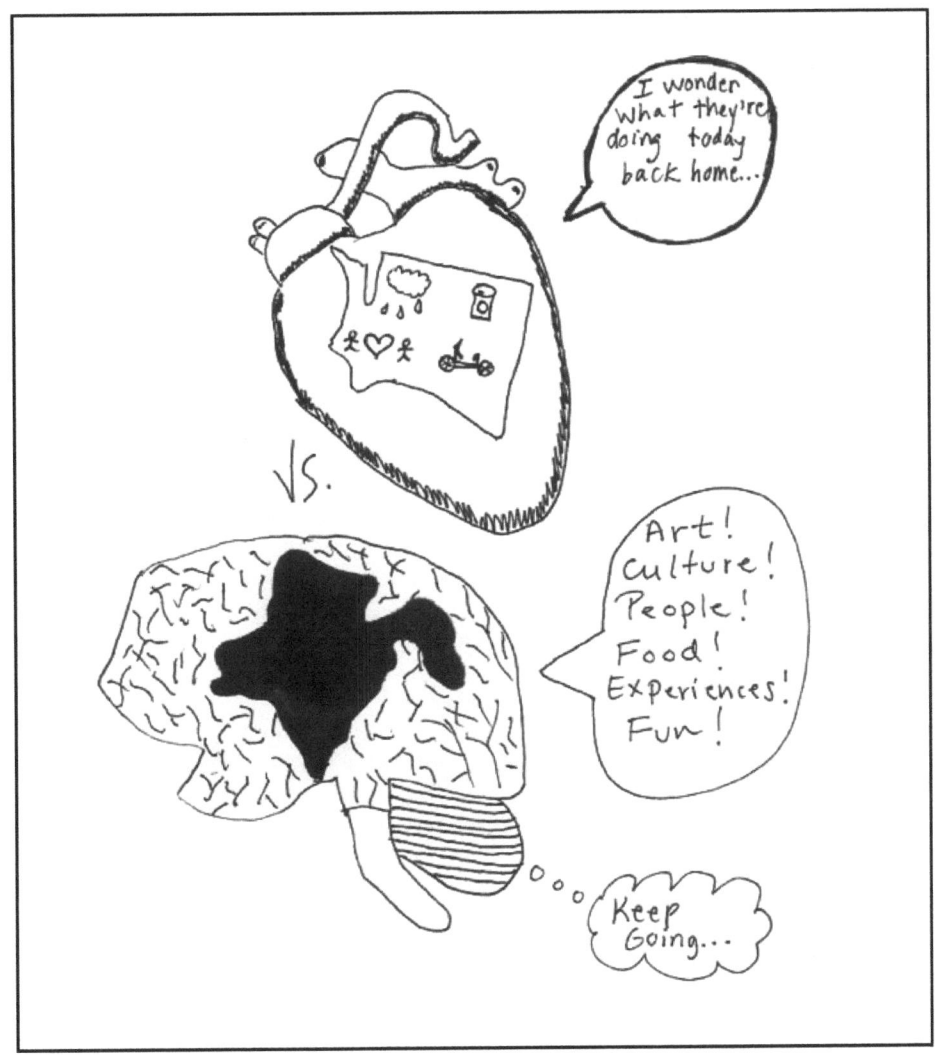

Often as you travel somewhere new for long periods of time, you begin to feel like you are missing out on what you left behind at home despite the amazing opportunities before you in a new place. Travel is essentially a battle between the heart and the brain, and when the brain wins out, it tells you to keep going despite your fears and hesitations. -Stefanie

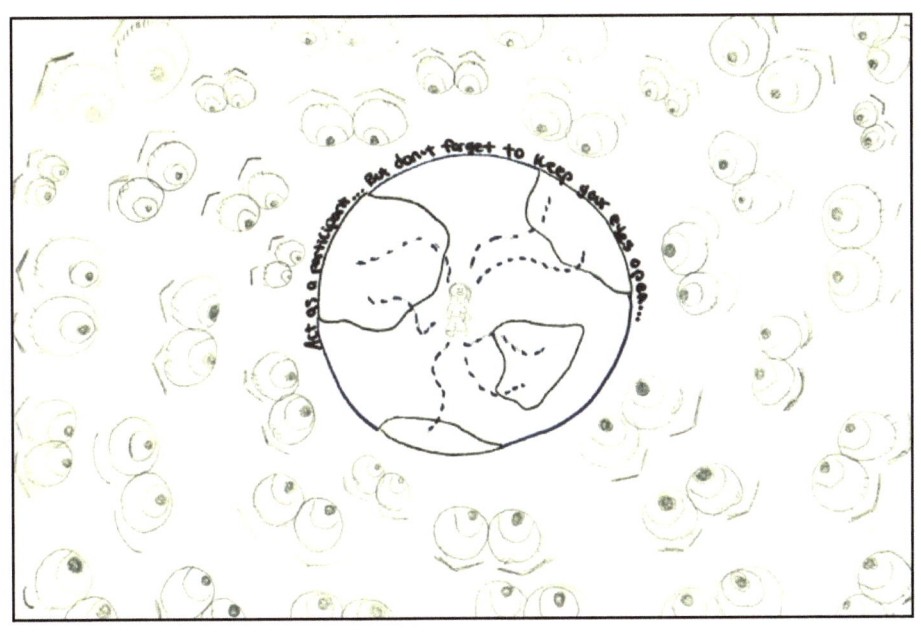

The eyes surrounding the world demonstrate that the person is being constantly watched and perceived in different manners as they travel to different places around the world. This is an integral aspect of traveling because it is important to not only learn about the places you are traveling to, but also to pay attention to your interactions and how local people are affected by outsiders immersing into their everyday lives.
-Meili

This image is based on my idea of "self" while abroad. During my time in India, I learned about how sensitive I am to my surroundings. This WOW represents my struggle with an "adaptable" identity amidst varying seasons of my life. -Trent

Dying of altitude sickness in your tent at nearly 6,000 meters is a scary experience, but navigating daily life alone in a foreign country can be equally confronting, even in a place like Nepal known for warmly welcoming visitors. If you get into serious trouble, is anyone there to hear your cries for help? -Ian

I hope to be global citizen with an open, balanced mind, peace in her belly, and love in her heart. This image inspires me to practice walking with mindfulness, acting from love, and giving kindness to those around me in each moment, wherever I am in the world.
-Ruby

If we think of a journey as a kite blowing wildly in the wind, as something that you must hold on to tightly while accepting its flow, we can think of exploration as both a thrilling and terrifying experience. Not knowing exactly where our minds may end up along the way, we must be prepared for the unexpected twists and turns that will inevitably appear. -Haley

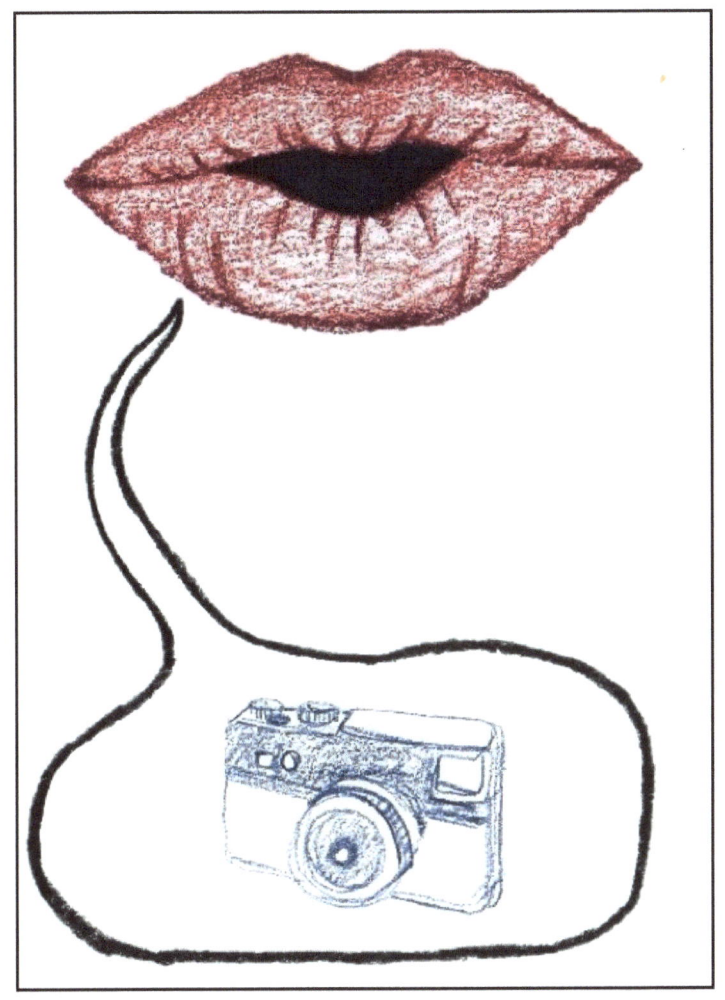

While we were in India, I had a hard time describing my experiences to people at home- and why they were already so impactful. Whenever I wanted people to understand our trip, I'd get flustered and just send them pictures so they could virtually share my experiences without me having to figure out how to articulate the complexity of our travels. -Liv

Price tags don't show you the true value it took to make your Gucci purse or Prada sunglasses. The intersections between global ethics and fashion run deeper and more raw, with every credit card swipe. -Karan

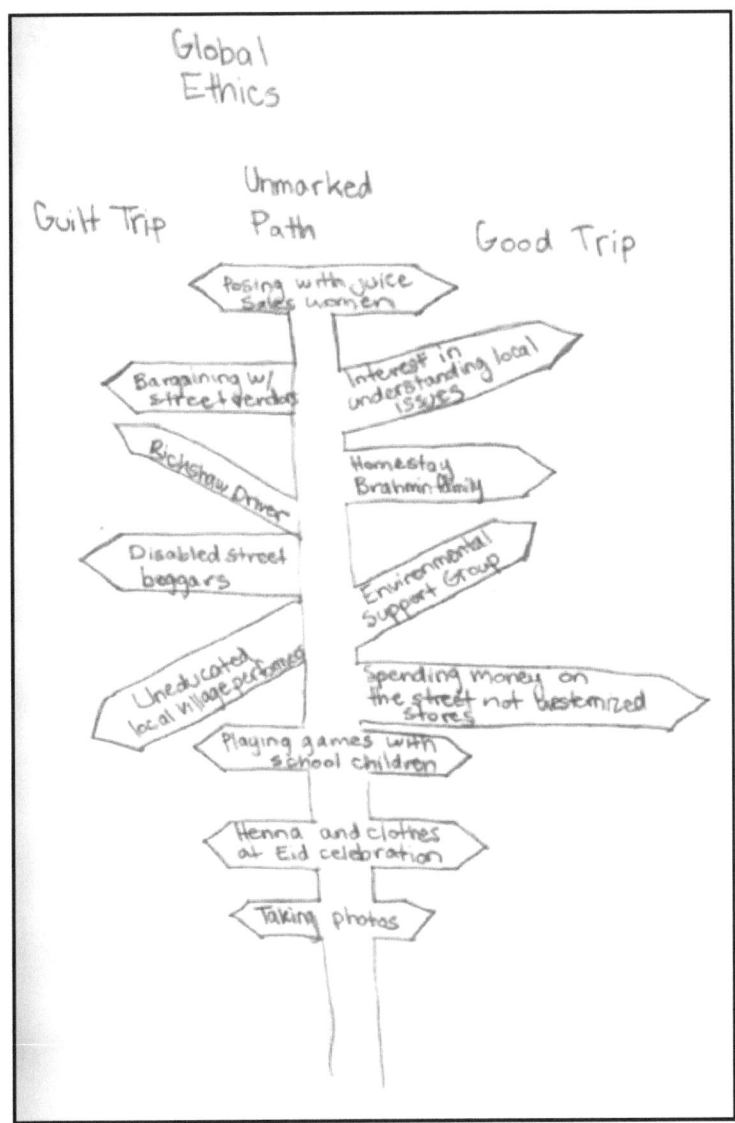

Along the "Unmarked Path" of global ethics, one can either go on the "Guilt Trip" or on the "Good Trip." As I recalled the many experiences from my trip, I tried to categorize them as things that I felt uncomfortable about or that I felt proud of. Some moments can't be clearly defined as one path or the other. -Miranda

To me, conducting myself in a foreign environment involves a degree of adaptability — which means knowing the difference between "getting lost" in a Western European city versus getting lost in Bangkok. When we're presented with the opportunity "to go", I think we absolutely should take it, but at the same time, I think it's important to let go of the expectations we have of what it means "to go." -Rikki

To turn someone's life upside down: to change someone's life completely, often in a way that is shocking or upsetting. Something you saw, something you learned, something you came to realize- suddenly something has changed in you.
-Chloe

Privilege is a sticky subject. Sometimes we don't even realize the privileges we've been afforded. Do we choose to ignore it, hide it or embrace it? Can we share it? What are you supposed to do with your privilege? -Spencer

Reflections: How We Unpack

Art by Elysse

When we come home from our travels abroad, our minds sometimes rest neither here nor there. Unpacking then, is not just about the literal emptying of a suitcase, but rather the unpacking of our memories. How do we reconcile our journeys abroad with our more local lives? Coming home means reacquainting ourselves with what was once familiar, sifting through our identities, and finding ways to integrate the here with the there. So now what? Let the unpacking begin.

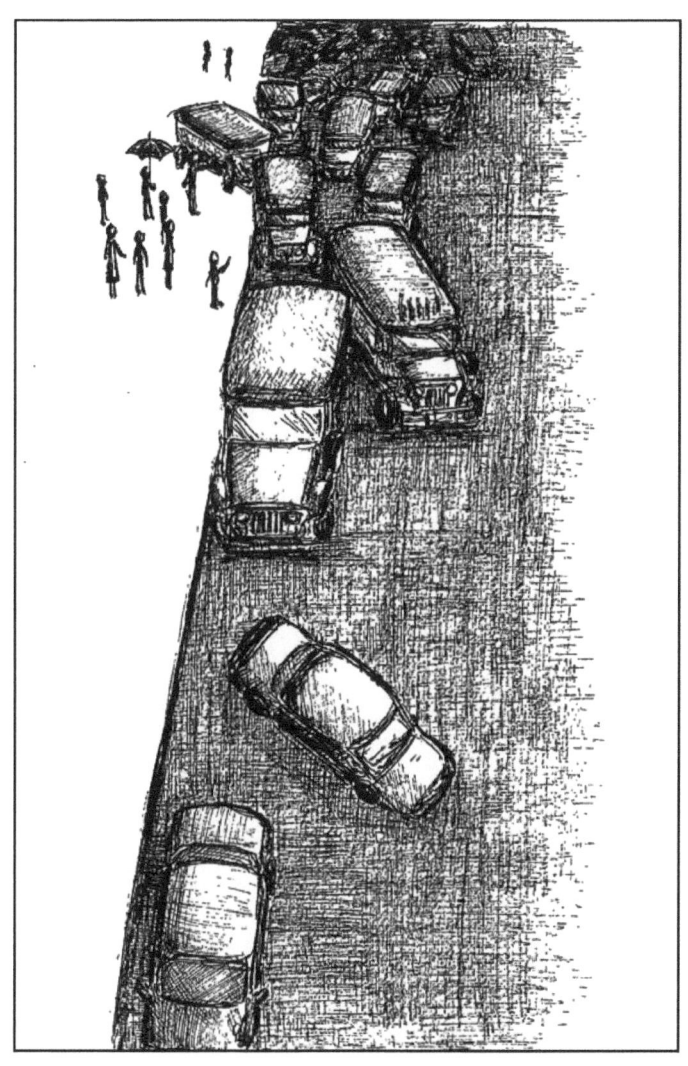

In Manila, I was shocked by the sheer amount of traffic that constantly congests the major highways, but perhaps more shocking was coming home to find myself the very next day tenderly rear-ending the car in front of me as I tried to parallel park along a quiet suburban two-lane arterial.
-Rikki

Coming home, I didn't know where to begin or how my friends would relate to my stories. I appreciated the people who were willing to ask thought provoking questions. I wanted to tell them how my experiences shaped my perspective and opinions since getting home. -Miranda

I think what surprised me the most about "coming home" was how easy it was. I expected to be horrified by America (and I am, a lot of the time), but I was honestly just content to be coming home. This is where I was raised, and I shouldn't feel obligated to feel any particular way upon returning, simply in the name of social justice. It's okay to sometimes care about burgers. -Liv

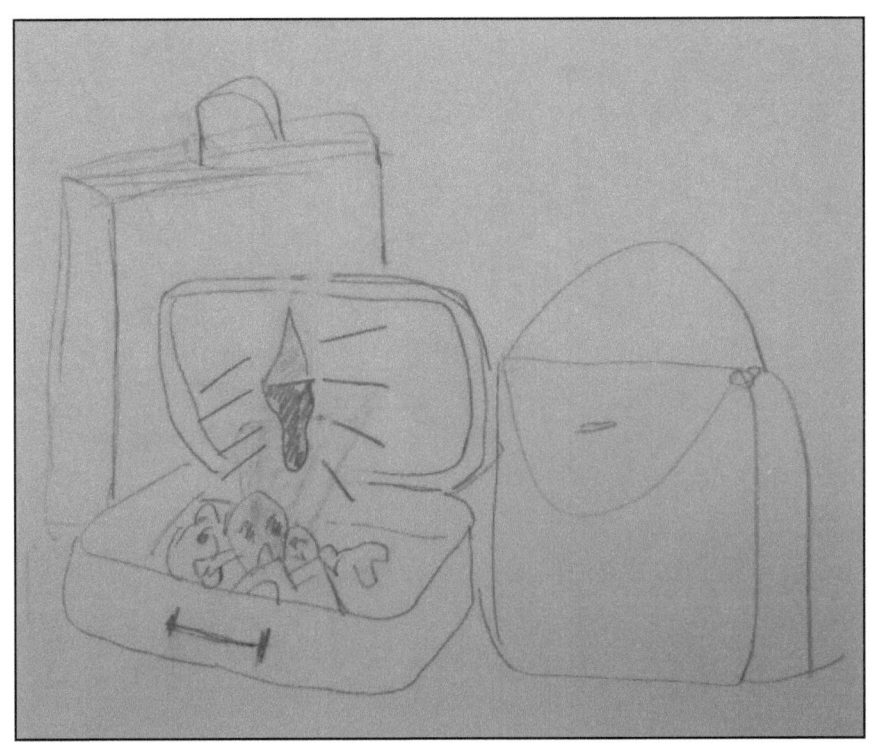

"No I do not weep at the world— I am too busy sharpening my oyster knife." Zora Neale Hurston wrote this in her essay "How it Feels to Be Colored Me." This is what unpacking was for me—it was staring into the dirt and rubble of injustice I had experienced, witnessed, or caused and not allowing myself be consumed by it. Even in the face of injustice, the world is still my oyster. -Zena

Coming home after being abroad is an experience that brings about a mixture of unfamiliarity and familiarity. In this WOW, I chose to illustrate the concept that the place that I once knew as home became meshed with an expanded understanding of home from the experience of studying abroad. My home here and my home abroad, while disparate are still closely connected through my view and experience of them.
-Elysse

My mind is like a computer chip, with well-worn paths and neat circuitry. India was a bowl of spicy, rich palak paneer dumped on my hard drive, an overload of sensory and intellectual information I didn't know how to process. It's still reconfiguring my wiring. -Anna

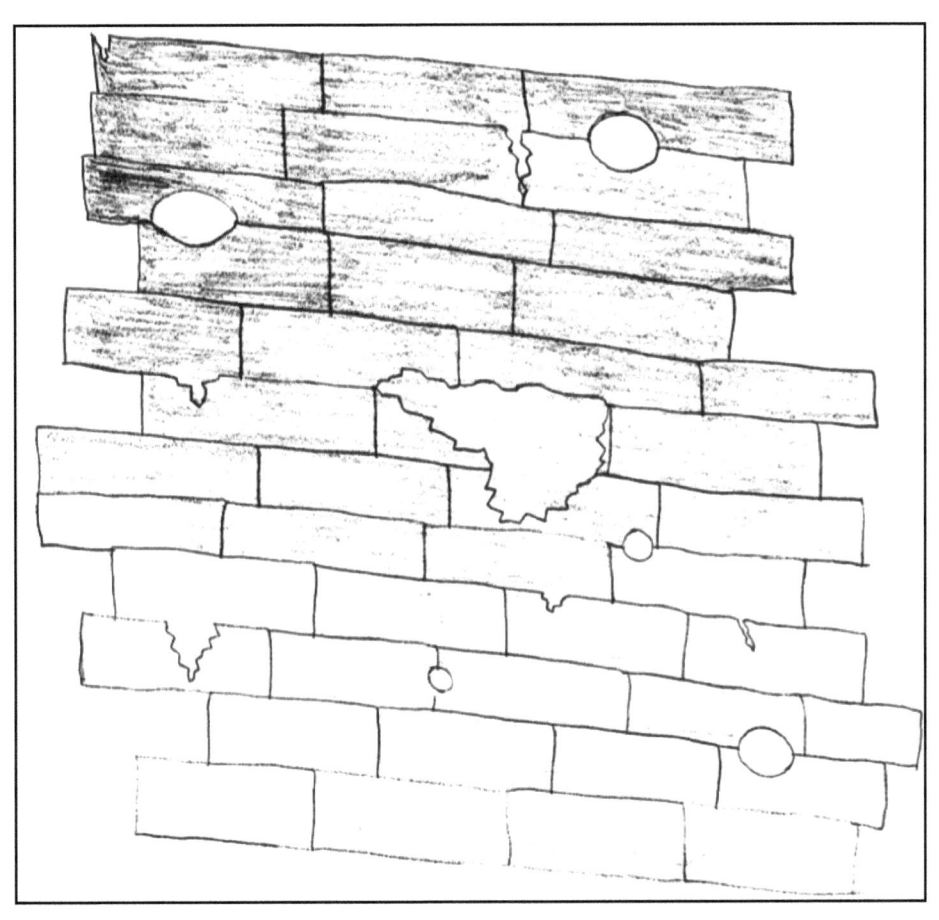

Each block represents a memory. The empty circles and jagged areas are the missing or unpleasant memories. All parts of the structure are added together to form who we are today.
-Miranda

The word "memory" reminded me of how women are seen as vessels of our cultures through the preservation of narratives. Storytelling and oral history are such an integral part of culture because they give people memories of things they never even experienced. -Liv

In the Philippines, we stayed with my friend's Lola who shared with us not only the secrets to her cooking, but also to her life, and perhaps one of the most important things she had shown us is to feed the people around you to feed yourself. -Rikki

These pages hold words and drawings that are tied to feelings, they are tied to experiences, and they are tied to memories. They are tied to reality that once was, but one that will continue to form and influence my tomorrow. -Karan

The memories of our experiences abroad are like the pictures we hang on our walls: moments from our past frozen in time that we constantly revisit and read, just as we attempt to situate ourselves within an ever-evolving present. -Ian

Coming home was an experience all in itself. The contrast of home and where I had just been was overwhelming. Everything was a big deal: how much food and fresh water I saw wasted, how much space existed between cars and how fast they went. The price of coffee blew my mind daily since I was still stuck converting dollars to rupees.
-Chloe

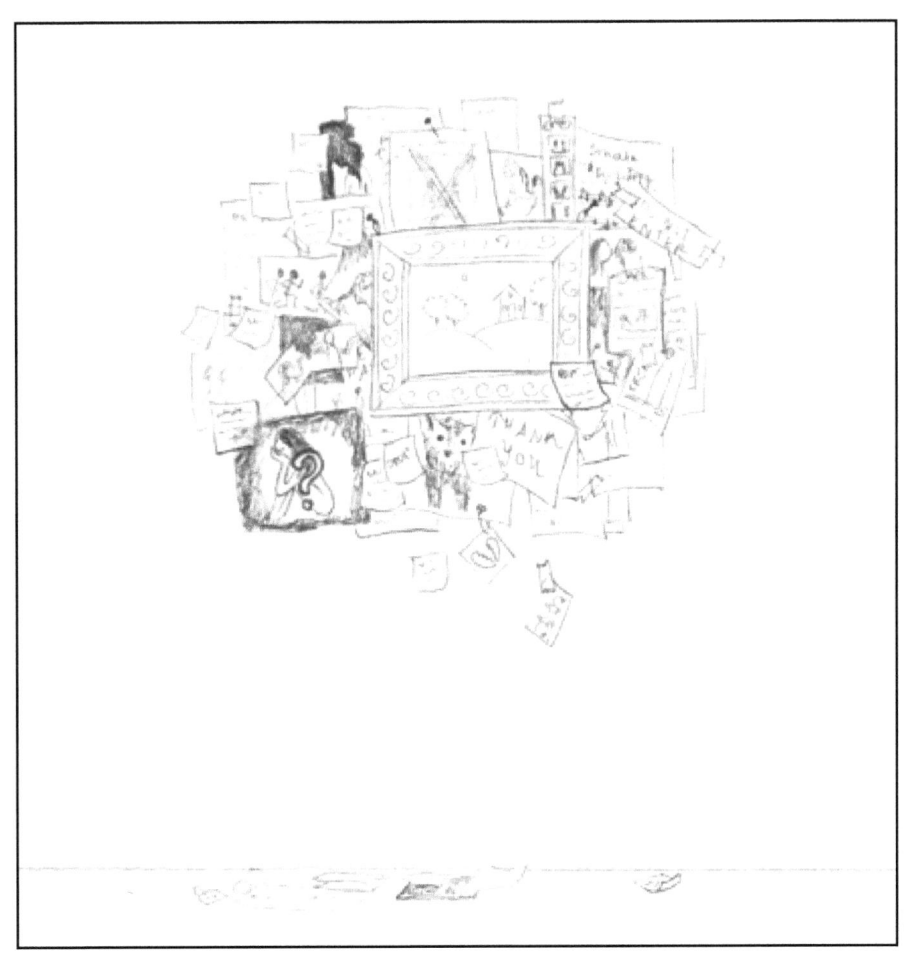

I imagine memory as being a collection of moments— images, words and emotions— that are constantly layered on top of each other as each new one is experienced. It's a jumbled, confusing mess, but it carries deep meaning and importance for our lives.   -Maya

What now? I'm back to what I thought was home. Should I continue like nothing ever happened, or should I be a new and improved version of myself? Everything is the same, but different at the same time. All I want to do is combine these divergent experiences without losing myself. -Spencer

WHAT ELSE MIGHT WE WOW ABOUT?

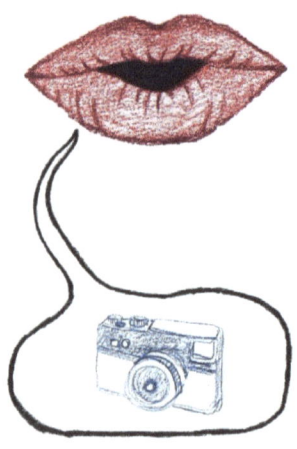

While our book revolves around travel as its central theme, WOWs are versatile. We can WOW just about any topic that we'd like to spend some time considering, reflecting upon, or unpacking. In this section, we've assembled WOWs that demonstrate a range of topics. In the next few pages you'll see we've WOWed about creativity, coming of age, the fluidity of space, animal studies, awareness, balance, and the act of questioning. Now it's your turn. What will you WOW about?

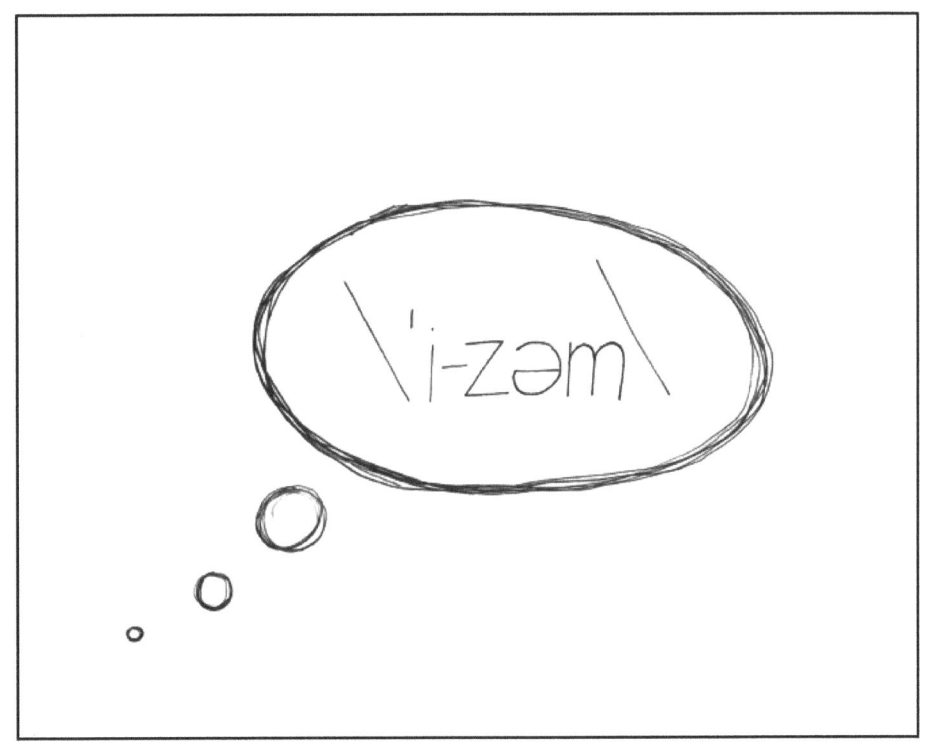

We see in pictures, think in words, and understand in definitions. Each layer of meaning becomes more abstract, until sometimes it's hard to see the reality the abstraction seeks to explain. -Anna

To understand creativity, I took the definition of the word and used it within a new medium for me: a comic strip. This comic is about the typical story of a person who thinks they cannot "art" when in actuality, the ability is within them as long as they attempt and do not become paralyzed by their own judgments.
-Stefanie

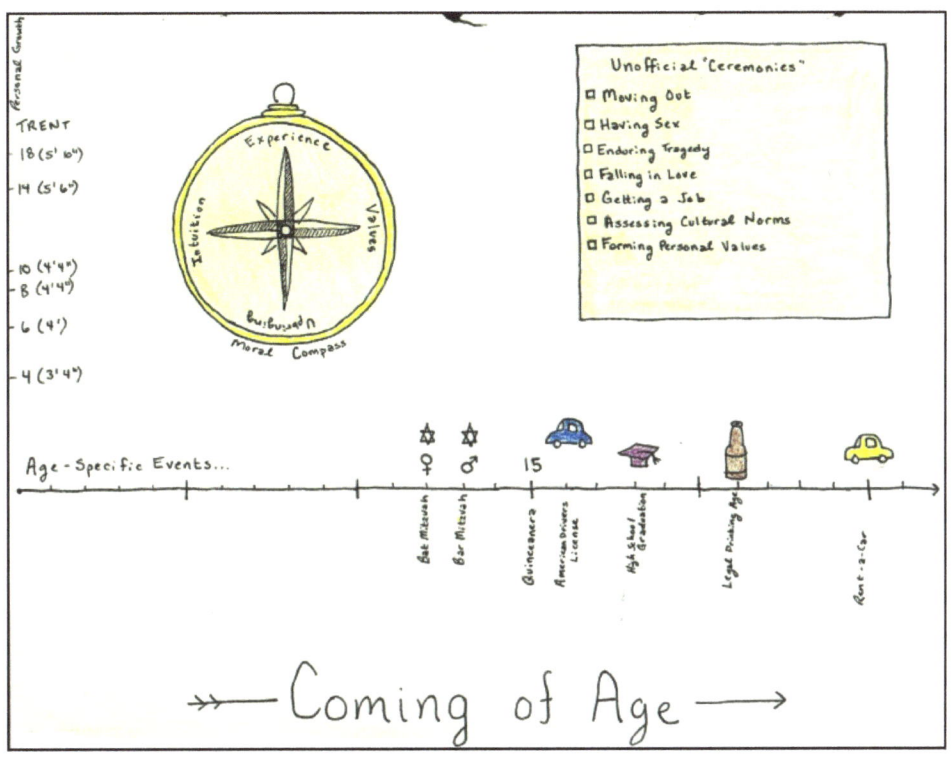

This WOW explores the idea of "coming of age" through brainstorming ways that different cultures mark maturity and celebrate rites of passage. This time of growth includes developing a personal moral compass, experiencing life events that hold cultural significance, and creating a timeline of ritualistic ceremonies that represent responsibility or adulthood. -Trent

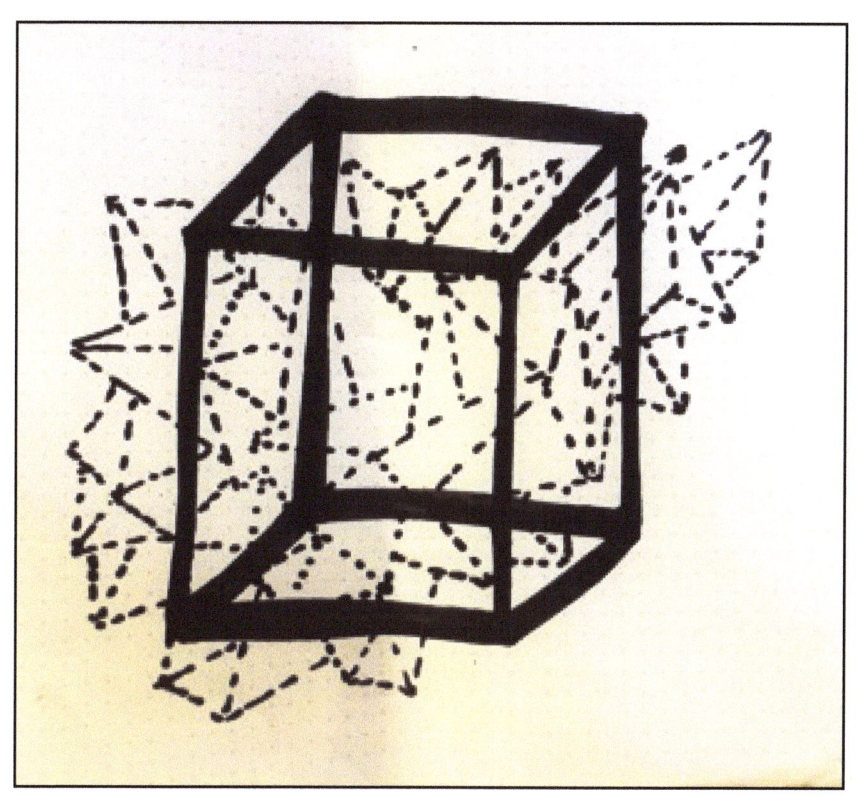

Space, both physical and not, is an important concept to consider when thinking about travel and new places. My WOW illustrates the way in which one space can hold an infinite amount of spaces within it. In other words, spaces are fluid in the sense that they change with context and the interaction we have with them.
-Elysse

Stray cats and dogs roam the city of Lima, but they're practically invisibilized by the humans that dominate this shared space. Why do we have such narrow views of sight, leaving so much unseen? How can we start to think beyond the human? -Haley

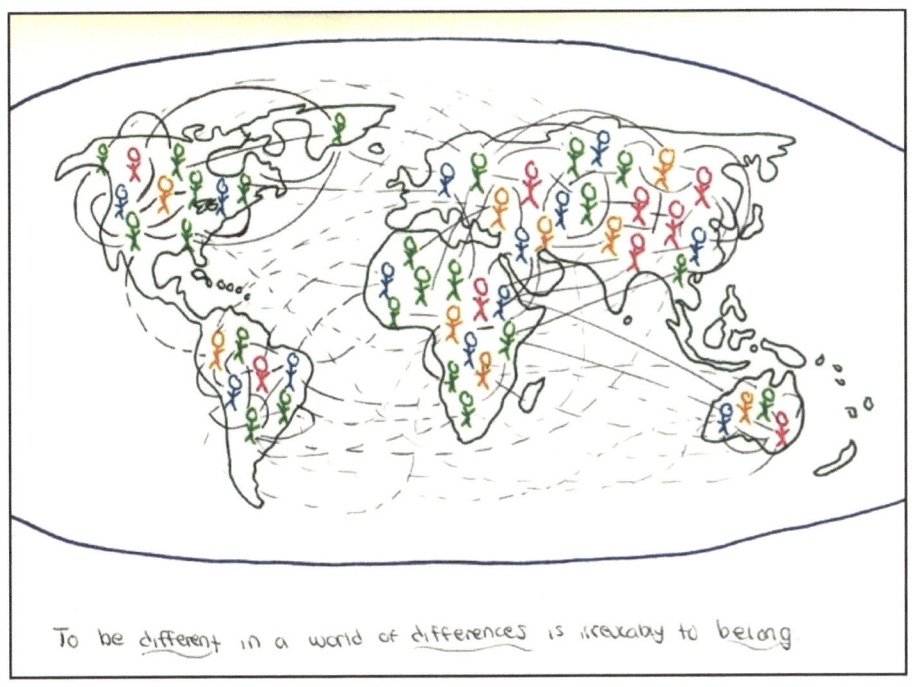

Having a reticulate consciousness - an awareness of oneself as part of an extensive network of the globe's inhabitants - is valuable when traveling both at home and in a new place. It is too common for people to see other populations as separate from themselves when immersing in another culture, but having a reticulate consciousness allows one to recognize and understand the relevance of cultural differences in relation to one's own life and actions. -Meili

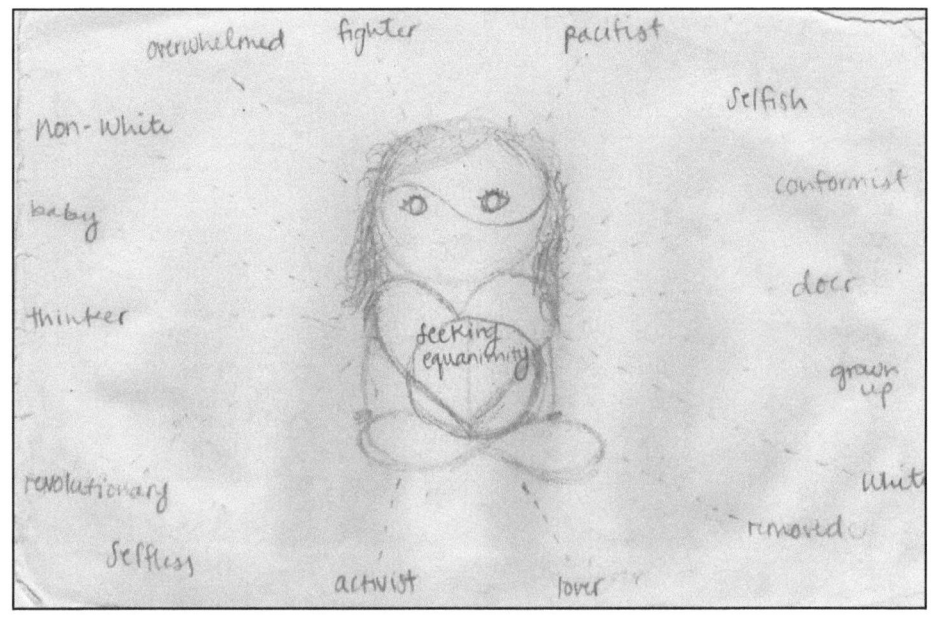

This self-portrait depicts my struggle to find balance amidst the intersections of my own identity. This process involves merging and reconciling these different aspects of self to create a holistic sense of self. My hair is frizzy and frazzled by both the humidity of India and the conflict of internal strife. -Ruby

The Unexpected Questions: How, What, Why. My travel abroad program wasn't as carefree as the dream of travel is made out to be, but hard questions never made my magic carpet ride any less magical. The Unexpected Questions made my study abroad experience meaningful on a level I never expected travel to hit. -Chloe

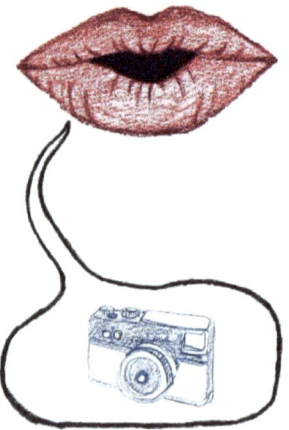

Thank you:

Cover image: Liv
Design Team: Elysse, Karan & Trent
Editing: Anna, Haley, Ian, Karan, Meili, Ruby, Rikki & Trent

Amy Hirayama, Bangalore Program Assistant

At the University of Washington, Seattle:
The Comparative History of Ideas Program,
UW Study Abroad Office

Shirin Subhani and Sasha Duttchoudhury with Unbodied Design for editorial and layout support

Our Global Partners:
Colleagues & friends in Amsterdam, Bangalore, Lima, Kathmandu, and Manila

Meet the WOWers

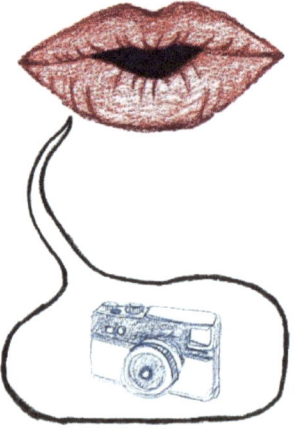

Stefanie Gonzalez (Bangalore, India)
Stefanie's academic focus and passion is bridging social justice and the arts. She is a Community, Environment and Planning major and a Gender, Women and Sexuality Studies minor. She is a proud Washingtonian, an avid concert-goer, a very big fan of dogs, and loves a good cup of coffee... or five.

Maya Norton (Bangalore, India)
Maya is a sophomore studying Comparative History of Ideas and pursuing a career in Physical Therapy. When she is not puzzling over her chemistry and biology classes, you will probably find her playing piano, trying to dance like Beyonce or eating sushi.

Trent Cayce (Bangalore, India)
Trent studies both Communications and Comparative History of Ideas, using his degrees to explore media representation and American rites of passage. A Texas native and Seattle transplant, he enjoys board games, scenic runs, discussing Myers Briggs (INFJ), and Fox Searchlight films. He would probably be a Hufflepuff.

Miranda Eriksen (Bangalore, India)
Miranda is studying public health and nutritional sciences. Not only is she immensely passionate about these topics, she also has a growing curiosity for social justice issues. Outside of her school life, Miranda is known for her love of hot yoga and appreciation for a tasty meal.

Liv Gee (Bangalore, India)
Liv is a senior majoring in Law, Societies, and Justice, with several minors that she keeps forgetting to declare. She spends most of her time baking and eating cookies, discussing the ecological factors associated with racial inequality, and panicking about who the Oakland A's will trade next.

Haley Bosco Doyle (Lima, Peru)
HBD is a fanatic of colorful patterns, white-tailed deer, and 1960s karaoke. Despite her parents' wishes, she studies the intersections between holistic health and artistic expression. Her laugh has been described as warmly infectious, a quality she strives to maintain throughout her life.

Karan Grewal (Bangalore, India)
Karan studies molecular biology and comparative history of ideas. He is passionate about the intersections of health, law, identity, and toothpaste. Karan enjoys hanging out with friends, watching all the related videos to the youtube video he's watching, and brewing hot masala chai on cold winter mornings.

Anna Mikkelborg (Bangalore, India)
Anna is a Washington native who wakes up early and stays up late. She is a social science student, a singer, and a newly minted traveler. Her adventures are fueled by peanut butter and good companionship.

Elysse Feigenblatt
(Amsterdam, Netherlands)
Elysse is a Visual Communication Design major in her Junior year. She is originally from Los Angeles, California but plans to stay in the Pacific Northwest after graduation. When not in class, she works part time as a barista and DJs for the school's radio station.

Ruby Lee (Bangalore, India)
Ruby is a senior majoring in Comparative History of Ideas, with minors in Education/Learning/Societies, and Diversity. Catch this self-proclaimed "Queen of Boba" jamming to a rad mix of reggae, girly tween hits, and nineties classics, helping people to see they are stars and passionately advocating love as a platform for positive social action.

Spencer Vale (Amsterdam, Netherlands)
Spencer is a senior majoring in Comparative History of Ideas. When he's not watching food network, you can usually find him sitting in front of his heater during the winter months. When he's not in hibernation, he might be pretending he's good at painting or trying to make the world a better place.

Ian Bellows (Nepal, India, & Tibet)
Ian Bellows is a junior in the Henry M. Jackson School of International Studies. From November 2014 to July 2015, he conducted solo fieldwork investigating the social, political, and economic drivers of Himalayan trekking and mountaineering. His research interests include critical development studies, civil society, foreign aid, relational poverty, ecotourism, and adventure travel.

Rikki Tsoi
(The Philippines, Thailand, & Malaysia)
Rikki is a sophomore intending to major in Biology. Some of her curiosities lie in environmental conservation and in the intersections between art and science. Her pipedream would be to become an entomologist, but in the meantime, she likes to spend her Yung Life rock climbing, tide pooling, and going to the off-leash park to play with dogs that aren't hers.

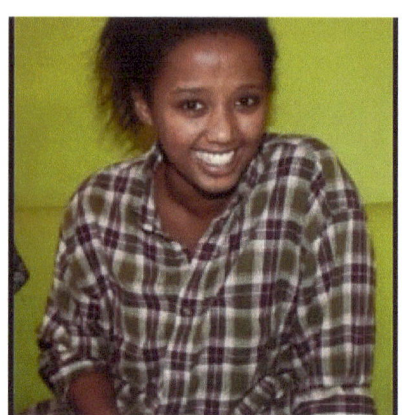

Zena Getachew (Bangalore, India)
Zena is a student, writer, and self-proclaimed breakfast sandwich connoisseur based in Seattle. She spends her free time with family, reading, and exploring hole in the ground restaurants. She (mistakenly) attributes her frequent— if not relentless— misuse of idioms to her being the daughter of Ethiopian immigrants.

Meili Powell (Bangalore, India)
With the intention of pursuing a career in teaching, Meili is a junior majoring in Early Childhood & Family Studies, and minoring in Education/Learning/Society and History. Outside of class, Meili enjoys listening to live music, going for runs through the rain, and searching for good food and memories with friends.

Chloe Sismour (Bangalore, India)
An artist, a baker, a concert-goer, and a free spirit, Chloe's days are spent meeting new people and searching for the best coffee around. She is pursuing art during her second year at university, and loves working through a new challenge.

www.ingramcontent.com/pod-product-compliance
Lightning Source LLC
Chambersburg PA
CBHW041805160426
43191CB00004B/59